Earth

by Martha E. H. Rustad

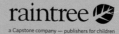

a Capstone company — publishers for children

Raintree is an imprint of Capstone Global Library Limited, a company incorporated in England and Wales having its registered office at 264 Banbury Road, Oxford, OX2 7DY – Registered company number: 6695582

www.raintree.co.uk
myorders@raintree.co.uk

Edited by Erika L. Shores
Designed by Juliette Peters and Katelin Plekkenpol
Picture research by Tracy Cummins
Production by Katy LaVigne
Originated by Capstone Global Library
Printed and bound in China.

ISBN 978 1 4747 1249 1

19 18 17 16 15
10 9 8 7 6 5 4 3 2 1

British Library Cataloguing in Publication Data
A full catalogue record for this book is available from the British Library.

Acknowledgements
We would like to thank the following for permission to reproduce photographs:
NASA: NOAA/GSFC/Suomi NPP/VIIRS/Norman Kuring, 9; Shutterstock: AstroStar, 5, cigdem, 7, Denis Tabler, cover, 1, Kalenik Hanna, Design Element, Lucian Coman, 19, momanuma, 17, Mopic, 11, PaulPaladin, 13, sebikus, 15, Sergey Novikov, 21.

Every effort has been made to contact copyright holders of material reproduced in this book. Any omissions will be rectified in subsequent printings if notice is given to the publisher.

All the internet addresses (URLs) given in this book were valid at the time of going to press. However, due to the dynamic nature of the internet, some addresses may have changed, or sites may have changed or ceased to exist since publication. While the author and publisher regret any inconvenience this may cause readers, no responsibility for any such changes can be accepted by either the author or the publisher.

Editor's Note
In this book's photographs, the sizes of objects and the distances between them are not to scale.

Contents

Our home

What is Earth?

A planet!

Planets orbit stars.

Planets are big and round.

Eight planets orbit the Sun.

Earth is third from the Sun.

Sun

Mercury

Venus

Earth

Mars

Jupiter

Saturn

Uranus

Neptune

Earth is almost
13,000 kilometres
(8,000 miles) wide.

9

Earth has three layers.

We live on the crust.

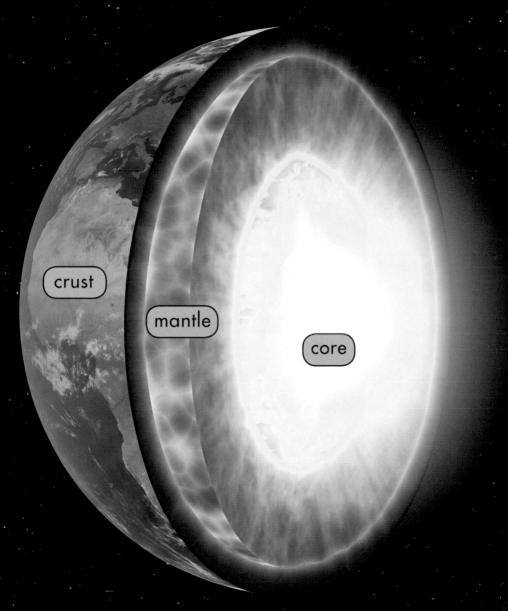

Moving

Earth spins each day.

The side facing the Sun has day.

The other side has night.

Sun

Earth

Moon

13

Earth orbits the Sun.

The trip takes one year.

Just right

The Sun warms Earth.

Earth is not too hot.

It is not too cold.

Plants and animals live on Earth.

We have water to drink.

We have air to breathe.

Earth makes
a good home.

Thank you, Earth!

Glossary

breathe   take air into and push it out of the lungs

core   centre; Earth's core is hot, liquid rock

crust   outer layer

layer   level of thickness that covers something

orbit   follow a curved path around an object in space

planet   large object in space that orbits a star

star   ball of burning gases; the Sun is a star

Find out more

Earth (Space), Charlotte Guillain (Raintree 2010)

Planet Earth (Beginners: Level 2), Leonie Pratt (Usborne, 2007)

Websites

resources.woodlands-junior.kent.sch.uk/revision/science/space.htm
Visit this website to find out more about Earth and space.

solarsystem.nasa.gov/planets/profile.cfm?Object=Earth
Learn facts about Earth on this website.

Index